I0022700

Pamela Chandler Colman

**Stories for Children**

A Book for Little Girls and Boys

Pamela Chandler Colman

**Stories for Children**
*A Book for Little Girls and Boys*

ISBN/EAN: 9783337005245

Printed in Europe, USA, Canada, Australia, Japan

Cover: Foto ©Thomas Meinert / pixelio.de

More available books at **www.hansebooks.com**

# STORIES FOR CHILDREN.

## A BOOK FOR

## ALL LITTLE GIRLS AND BOYS.

EDITED BY MRS. COLMAN.

NEW YORK:

HOWE & FERRY, 76 BOWERY.

1860.

Entered according to Act of Congress, in the year 1844,

BY P. A. COLMAN, BROOKLINE,

in the Clerk's Office of the District Court of Massachusetts

# CONTENTS.

# INNOCENCE.

## 1.

N infant child had passed **away,**
　　Where angels live and love, —
His heavenly Father wanted him,
　　And took him home above;
And happy was the child to find
　　A garden full of bowers,
Where many other children too,
　　Were playing with the flowers.

## II.

The lambs were skipping on the green,
   The trees were full of birds,
And fruit hung down deliciously,
   Above the grazing herds;
While music from a thousand throats
   Came warbling through the air,
And fragrance such as angels love,
   Blew from the flowrets fair.

## III.

Oh! what a lovely sight was that
   The little cherub saw,
And how it longed to frolic too,
   And wear the dress they wore;

For wreaths of flowers, like dazzling gold,
   And silver shining white,
Hung o'er their breasts and on their arms,
   So beautiful and bright.

# IV.

Just then an angel, fair to see,
   And shining like the sun,
Came smiling with a mother's smile,
   And blessed the little one;
While in her arms she took the child,
   And kissed it o'er and o'er,
And bade it play among the rest,
   In joy for evermore.

## V.

Away it ran with mirthful glee,
　To join the little band,
That round about soon gathered fast,
　And clasped their brother's hand;
Then crowning him with pretty flowers,
　They laughed with joy intense,
Because their hearts had felt no sin,
　And all was Innocence.

# THE FAIRY OF THE ROSE.

BY RUFUS DAWES.

CORINNE was a beautiful little girl, who always obeyed her parents, and who loved her brothers and sisters. She liked to walk about in the country, and to gather pretty flowers that grew in the fields, and sometimes she would stay out so late before the sun set, that the cows would go home before she did, and Letty, the housemaid, would be waiting for her with her silver porringer and supper.

One afternoon she was looking at the lovely clouds that were moving along under the blue sky, and one of them poured down a gentle mist, which made a brilliant rainbow.    Corinne had often seen rainbows from the parlor window, but now she saw one out in the open fields, and it seemed to her that it was close by, and was bending over a rose-bush.

"If I could only catch that beautiful rainbow!" said Corinne, and away she ran, with her bright curling hair streaming to the breeze, and her blue eyes shining like violets in the dew.

But Corinne soon found that the rainbow fled as fast as she pursued it; but as she passed by the rose-bush, she saw a young and handsome female, who seemed to be hiding among the roses, and was now looking out upon the child.

"My pretty little Corinne," said the female, "do n't run any more after the rainbow — you will never be able to overtake it. But stop a moment here by the roses. I am the Fairy of the Rose, and I love to make good little children happy. You may come here every day while the roses bloom, and carry one home with you in the evening. Take this," said she, offering a beautiful bud to Corinne ; "it is the emblem of innocence. Take it, sweet little Corinne, and remember the Fairy of the Rose. Be a good child, and you will be more beautiful than the flowers, and more delightful than the rainbows which you love."

Corinne thanked the fairy for the present, and away she scampered to her mother. And after that, she used to visit the rose-

bush every day, and while she played with
the butterflies and the humming-birds, the
Fairy of the Rose used to sing to her the
sweetest songs, and sometimes she would
fall asleep and dream such beautiful dreams,
that it would have made her mother's heart
beat with delight to see the angelic smile
on her lips.

In this way Corinne grew in favor with
all, for she always minded her lessons, and
obeyed her parents, and ever remembered
with affection the *Fairy of the Rose.*

# THE LAMMIE.

## A MODERN FAIRY TALE.

### BY MISS A. A. GRAY.

OSA went to bed weeping. It was a rainy night, and while the rain-drops pelted the window frames, Rosa's tears fell upon her pillow. She had been a disobedient girl, and her mother had reproved her more severely than usual, and so Rosa wept, not in penitence because she had done wrong, but in displeasure and impatience because she had been punished, and she said to herself, "It is too bad! Mother is cruel, I am sure she is, and she does not love me, I know she does not."

Pitiable feelings and thoughts were these to
go to sleep upon — bad stuff for dreams
to be woven of; but Rosa did fall asleep
while her breast was thus disquieted.  She
dreamed, and in her dream she stood by
the border of a pond.  She bent over, and
looked into the water; but the water reproved her, by showing her the distorted
features of a weeping girl.  She started
back, and in anger threw a stone into the
face of the reprover, for presuming to speak
so plainly to her.  "There," said she, "you
cannot show me such a picture of myself
now, if you would; I have wrinkled your
own face well, for giving me such a portrait
of mine."  The honest reprover only smiled;
and while Rosa was watching the dimples
which she chose to call "wrinkles," she

heard, behind her, a sound as of rustling leaves, or of rain-drops pattering on the leaves. Was it the rain beating on the window, or the curtain fluttering, — was it the grasshoppers leaping about over the blackberry bushes? "Rosa," whispered a voice close behind her, which sounded as soft as the crunching of a crust of bread. Rosa turned her head around, and oh! there were the black elves, close beside her; those elves that dwell (if I say truly) in the hollow of the earth. Spider-like little creatures they were, very black, and with long slender limbs, which they threw about in a most fantastic manner, and with large owlish eyes, which they seemed to think were made on purpose to be rolled from side to side. "Rosa," said one of the elves, which seemed

2

to be the king, " do not believe what that
pond says; I know his tricks.  He always
was given to telling falsehoods; believe me,
he is a wrinkled sinner.  You are a good
child, and your face is a pretty one.  Come,
we love you; come with us; we have a fine
home."  And he reached out his claw-hand,
and took hold of Rosa's hand, and it felt to
Rosa as if she had clasped a branch of a
rough-barked shrub.  And with the spider-
like troop she swept along, over hills, plains,
rivers, and seas; and then they all dashed
headlong down into a deep dell, at the bottom of which was a bed of dry leaves.  The
elf-king scratched the leaves away with his
claw-feet, throwing them up till the air was
full.  When he had scratched them away,
a hole was discovered in the earth, not much

larger than a squirrel's hole. " There,"
said the elf, " is our stair-way; go down,
Rosa; here we will feast you well, and give
you a mirror, which shall tell you the truth."
And he went down the spiral staircase, draw-
ing Rosa after him, and the whole troop
followed, with a sound like an army of cock-
roaches, making a more hasty than dignified
retreat from the store-room. Down, down,
down they wound and wound till it seemed
to Rosa they must be near the other side
of the earth — millions of miles — many
days, it seemed. Oh, that wearying staircase! Yet they went swiftly, for it is easy
to go down stairs, every one knows. Before they had reached the bottom, Rosa's
brain was in such a whirl that she was
scarcely conscious of anything. Suddenly

she felt an electric shock, which seemed to bring her to consciousness. It was the floor of the great elfin hall which her feet had touched. And now she was whirled around in a dance with the band of elves, and it seemed as if she could not help dancing on the electric floor. In the midst of the hall burned a smoky fire, and over the fire a caldron hung from the ceiling, and the smoke from the fire, and the steam from the caldron hung in heavy clouds around.

" Supper is not ready yet," said the elf-king, who still held Rosa's hand clasped in one of his claws, while he ran the other up through his hair, which was as sleek and soft as the down of a porcupine. " We shall have time for a little conversation before supper. Now tell me your offence.

I heard your mother's voice scolding you;
but I do not know what it was for."

"I went away secretly," said Rosa, "to
see one of my schoolmates, when my mother
had forbidden it, and when she punished
me I was angry, and I am now, for mother
is cruel to me."

"Never mind what your mother says to
you, my dear," said the elf; and he went
on and gave a long lecture, which thoroughly
persuaded Rosa that she was nothing more
or less than an innocent and injured child.
"Come now, the soup is ready," said the
elf. And all the elves stood round the caldron, each with his ladle. And Rosa had
a ladle too, and she feasted with the elves.

The soup tasted good; but shortly she
began to feel faint and sick, and so dizzy

that she could not stand; and at length
went into convulsions, of which she was all
the time conscious; presently it seemed as
if she could no longer use her limbs, nor
could she sit up nor stand, neither lie in
any way except upon her face, and at last
it was as if she had no limbs; but she could
move her body very easily, and it seemed
to grow longer and longer, as she lay upon
the floor, and she loved to move about,
this side and that; but still she could not
stand erect. "What has happened to me,"
thought she, and she asked the elf king to
show her the truth-telling mirror. "Come,"
said he; and she followed him, moving along
on the smooth floor with the most delightful
ease.

The elf led her to a basin of black look·

ing liquid; she looked into it, and there, in the blackness, she beheld herself transformed into — oh what? a white and woolly lamb. " Oh," said she, " this is a true mirror ; but why is it that I cannot skip and play ? It is quite as pleasant, though, to glide about on this smooth floor." After some time, she had become so much accustomed to believing herself a lamb, that it really began to be as if she ran and leaped about, and presently she seemed to be running up the spiral staircase, and when she had reached the top, she seemed to spring along over the meadows, thinking to herself, Oh! now what will mother say, when she sees I am an innocent lamb? Yes, I am a lamb! Oh, the truth-telling mirror.

" The truth-telling mirror ! " repeated a

soft, sweet voice directly in front of Rosa. It seemed to come from amongst the high clover through which she was bounding, as she thought, but she saw nothing but the red clover blossoms and the yellow king-cups. Hist! she hears the gentle waving of wings, like the wings of doves; and from out the clover arise beautiful little fairy-like forms, bright as humming-birds. "Rosa," said one of them, in a voice like the Æolian harp, "Come, I will show you the truth-telling mirror. I have it up in my pavilion in the sky. We are the fairies of the upper air; I am the queen. I have, resting on the clouds, a pavilion made of pearl. Oh! it is light up there; you cannot look around but the rainbow meets your eye."

"I have looked into the true mirror,"

said Rosa, "and it showed me the lamb which thou seest I am."

"My eye sees thee but as the child Rosa; but my heart knows thy heart as the mirror would show it, and I know what thou art. Follow me; it is best thou shouldst see thyself."

"Give me thy hand," said Rosa, "and lead me up."

"Nay, I cannot give thee my hand; I would not willingly come very near such as thou; but thou shalt be led. We fairy band will collect, and unite together, and a golden cloud shall enwrap us, and the cloud shall rise up, and thou shalt follow it till it reaches the pavilion."

"I do not love you; you are not kind," said Rosa; "but I am curious to look into

3

your mirror; so I will follow." And Rosa
saw the cloud arise like a globe of gold, and
she seemed to arise with it; and in circles
up they swept, higher! higher! till, as she
saw the golden ball above and the green
ball of earth below, the latter seemed the
smaller globe of the two.

When they had reached the pavilion, the
fairies came out of the cloud and alighted
upon the pearly steps, and it seemed to
Rosa as if she had a flock of doves waving
their wings around and above her.

The queen led her into the pavilion, where
she saw a table on which a splendid feast
was spread. "I do not wish to eat with
you," said Rosa; "I only wish to see if
your mirror speaks the truth."

"Thou canst not eat with us," said the

queen; "we ask not such as thou to our table. Come, pitiable child! and behold thyself. My mirror shows not the outside, but the inside;" and the queen led Rosa to a crystal basin, wreathed with flowers of many hues, and sending forth the sweetest odors. The dome-roof of the pavilion was lined with sapphires, and this was reflected in the clear water, and on this blue ground Rosa beheld herself, — a scaly serpent of a dull coppery red. It recoiled at the sight of itself. "Oh, you are cruel!" she cried to the queen; "this cannot be true!" But she perceived again that she did not leap and run, nor stand erect, but moved along with an undulatory motion, and her ear seemed to hear the scaly folds sweep along as she moved. She hissed in anger and

writhed in agony, because she dreaded that
her mother should behold her in that form.
" Nay, my poor child," said the queen,
" this is vain; go and transform thyself
into something better."    And it seemed to
Rosa that she had awakened and found that
she was lying in bed, still retaining the
serpent form.    " Oh! agony! mother will
come into the chamber, and instead of her
Rosa, whom I know she means to forgive,
she will find a scaly serpent coiled up in
the bed.    And instead of the kiss she would
have given me, she will give a shriek, and
run frightened away."    Then Rosa thought
her mother came in, started and shrieked
as she had dreaded, and the poor child
arose as erect as she was able, and protested
she was not what she appeared.    " Mother!

mother!" she cried, "I am not a serpent! oh! I am not, believe me, mother! Forgive me! kiss me, and I shall be your Rosa again." "Kiss a serpent?" cried her mother, "Heaven have mercy! where is my child?" And then her mother with clasped hands looked upon her with a look that pierced her heart, and she sunk down and crept beneath the bed-clothes. Her mother shrieked — but no — it was the creaking of the chamber door. Rosa awoke — her mother bent over her and kissed her wet cheek. "What ails thee, my dear child? Why dost thou weep so?" "Mother! mother! I am not a serpent! do not kill me!" "My dearest child, what have you been dreaming about?" said her mother laughing; and Rosa now laughed in delight to find that she was not a serpent, and she told her dream. "Repent, my Rosa, and behave well to-day, and perhaps you will dream a pleasanter dream, to-night. Was it not the serpent within you which induced you cunningly to deceive me and to disobey me, for the sake of gratifying your own selfish wishes? Take care that he does not creep in again. Now dress yourself, and after breakfast I shall have some work for you to do, and if you do your task well, and are obedient and sweet-tempered all through the day, then I shall believe the serpent has crept away and a pretty lamb is born in you." Rosa felt very light-hearted when she laid down to rest the next night, for she had done so well during the day that her mother had hardly been obliged to reprove her for anything, which was remarkable, for Rosa was rather a wilful child. " What a good girl I have —— " but before the sentence was completed, Rosa was in a dream. It was not rainy that night, nor were the window curtains fluttering ; but Rosa heard the rustling and pattering behind' her as she stood by the pond, curling her ringlets around her fingers, and thinking how prettily she looked. " Rosa! Rosa! " said many cracked voices, " come and ride the peacock. Our peacock steeds will carry us up to the clouds, so that we can see the pavilion of the air-fairies. Come, we are all going up." And the elf-king touched with his wand some flowers that grew on the banks of the pond, and instantly they were changed into peacocks. Each of the elves leaped upon the back of one, and the king placed Rosa before him on his. This was certainly fine ; the peacocks spread their tails so wide and looked so proud, and held their pretty crowned heads so high; and though the elf king's claw grasped Rosa's waist râther tightly, and his voice grated harshly upon her ear, when he now and then cried, " high ! high, boy ! " to his steed, she did not much care for it, it was so fine to be sweeping through the air on the beautiful bird.

But look ! look ! what is coming ? An army of eagles ; and hark what flapping of wings ! From the clouds the troop seems to come ; the long quilled feathers of their far-spread wings glance like golden arrows in the sun; on the back of each bird is mounted one of the beautiful fairies of the upper air. The peacocks shut their tails and screamed in affright, and the golden eagles shrieked in defiance.

"Hence to your own dark domain!" cried the queen to the elfin band, as her royal bird pounced upon the king's peacock, while all the other eagle-mounted fairies were giving a downward chase to the elves. "Quarter! quarter!" cried the king in a voice which reminded one of a pair of tongs endeavoring to bring harp tones out of a gridiron. The eagle had grasped the peacock's head in his talons, and the poor bird struggled painfully. The king was hurled into the air, and followed his crown as it fell towards the earth, looking

like a spider grasping at her ball of eggs.
Rosa, too, slid from the smooth back of her
steed; but she was caught by the queen
and placed before her on the royal bird.

The eagle troop wheeled about, and ris-
ing in circles higher and higher, soon hov-
ered near the pavilion.  He on whose back
the queen and Rosa were mounted, alighted
on a golden ball which crowned the roof;
here he stood a moment, glancing up at the
sun, first with one eye, then with the other,
and turning his golden neck about and
quivering his great wings; then giving one
shout of grand joy, he arose and wheeling
about, softly descended and entered the
pavilion, alighted and stood still while the
queen dismounted with her charge.  " Now
let me eat with you, now let me look into

the mirror and behold myself," said Rosa. "The table is spread, thou seest," said the queen, "but thou canst not yet partake with us; but thou mayest look into the blue water, and see all thou canst see." And she led Rosa to the basin. And how Rosa's heart beat as she looked in and beheld herself as painted on the blue, in the form of a lamb, white and woolly; but oh! sad deformity! a lamb with a peacock's tail spread high over his head; what a monster was this. "Poor me," thought Rosa, "I am a thing fit to be exhibited in the museum. What if my parents should think fit to exhibit me there, just for a punishment, and then after I am dead, set me up among the stuffed animals. But why should I be punished? have I not repented and reformed? and why does this tail adhere to me? This mirror is not quite true," said she to the queen. "Thou hast done thy tasks well," said the queen, "but thou hast told both thyself and others of it; yes, thou hast boasted; thou hast not been humble in thy joy."

Presently it seemed to Rosa that she was in the museum, where a great concourse of people was collected, and all were staring at the lamb with a peacock's tail and pointing and laughing. And then she was in a menagerie, where the showman was compelling her to show herself off, making her spread wide the wonderful tail, and leap bars, and pace round with a monkey on her back, and do many other silly things. Poor Rosa, in her mortifications she almost wished herself a serpent again. Then she seemed to be at home and all her brothers and sisters laughed at the peacock's tail, and one of her brothers pulled some of the feathers out, and shook them in her face; but this she was glad to find was only one of her sisters who had come to awaken her, and was shaking a handkerchief in her face. "Be quiet, Charles!" cried Rosa, as she opened her eyes, "you are unkind to treat me so." "Is sister Ellen unkind to come and wake you to go to walk on this beautiful morning?" "Oh dear! dear! I thought it was Charley pulling my feathers out, and it hurt me." "Your feathers? why my silly chicken you are not yet fledged; come, downy nestling, up and dress, and let us go to walk." "I am a lamb, only—— but I will certainly be a lamb to-day."

The next night Rosa stood in her dream by the pond where she was plucking lilies, and as she reached over, her happy face was to be seen in the water, but she did not see it, so full was her mind of the fair lilies; while she was smelling of one, she heard at a distance behind her the black troop, and the king called in a voice that sounded like the creaking of a cork when being drawn from the bottle, "throw down those horrible lilies; their breath is death and destruction; we cannot come, we dare not approach till thou hast thrown them away; they hate us from the bottom of their wicked hearts."

"Dear lilies!" said Rosa, "then I will

keep you as a safeguard, for you love me,
I know you do; you say it with the sweet-
ness of your breath. Yes, you love me,
and I love you, and I will wear you in my
bosom." She placed them in her bosom,
and as she bent her head to smell of one,
she heard a very small voice, like the
Æolian harp-tones of the fairy queen; they
were so very faint, she thought they came
from a distance. She looked around and
above, but saw no fairies, nor elves neither,
for the black troop, seeing her cherish the
lilies, had vanished. The voice sounded a
little louder, and said, "Rosa, dear child!
love us and we will love you; do well, and
we will always be with you to guard you;
feel, think, or do ill, and you force us to
leave you." "Ah! is it the lily speaking?

the voice comes from amongst the yellow
central petals. No, it is the queen. She
rises up from her beautiful couch." "Wilt
thou go with me to the pavilion?" said she.
"Oh, take me with thee," said Rosa, "and
let me look into the blue mirror once
more." The queen touched the lily with
her wand, and it was an ivory car of light
and exquisite workmanship, and its cushions
were of cloth of gold. Three pair of white
doves were harnessed to it, and when Rosa
and the queen were seated upon the golden
cushions, the doves spread their wings, and
as they beat the air, making a soft waving
sound, onwards and upwards swiftly sped
the beautiful coach and six, and soon amid
the dove-colored clouds peered the dome-
roof and pearly pillars of the pavilion

Silently the car rolled along through the rounded clouds, and when it reached the steps of the pavilion the six gentle steeds closed their wings, and uncurling their red feet, stood with arched necks and blinking eyes, while Rosa and the queen alighted. The queen then touched the car with her wand, and again the lily was there. It lay at her feet, and she picked it up and placed it in Rosa's bosom. They entered the pavilion, where the feast was spread, and where the fairy train awaited the arrival of their queen. " See," said the queen, " I have brought you a pretty guest. Eat with us," said she to Rosa, " and then thou shalt go to the mirror." And Rosa sat down and ate with them, and then with a heart full of doubts and fears, yet throbbing

4

with joy and hope, she arose and went
to the flower-wreathed basin. Oh, happy
child! There on the sapphire ground was
the pure white lamb looking her in the
face, and no longer with the peacock's tail,
nor with any sign of the peacock about it;
but wearing about its neck a wreath of
beautiful flowers. The innocent lamb in
her heart now bounded with joy. "Dear
child,' said the queen, kissing her affection-
ately, "thou bearest the lamb in thy heart
now, because thou hast not only done thy
tasks well, but whenever a feeling of self-
praise endeavored to steal in, thou didst
strive to shut the door of thy heart against
it, and didst humbly pray to be delivered
from so deadly a foe to thine eternal
peace."

It seemed now to Rosa that she was in
her own chamber, still wearing the form of
a lamb, and she thought her mother came
in, and seeing a pretty lamb wreathed with
flowers, leaping about the chamber, smiled
and cried out, "Oh, pretty creature! where
didst thou come from?" And Rosa felt
so frolicsome that she thought she would
not tell who the lamb was, but ran up to
her mother, and went leaping around her,
and her mother caught the pretty lamb in
her arms, and warmly caressed it. Then
Rosa laughed to think how she was going
to surprise her mother, and the laugh
awoke her, and she laughed still more when
she found she was really in her mother's
arms. "Ah, what is so funny, my love?
have sweet spirits been with you in your
dream? As I came and bent over you, a

pleasant smile was on your lips, and when I kissed them, you laughed in your sleep." "Oh, mother, I am a lamb! a happy lamb, for see the garland around my neck;" and she put her hand to her neck, expecting to feel the flowers. "Ah, no, but it was a sweet dream mother, and it shall be a true one, for I will be a lamb." "Yes, my dearest," said her mother, "the lamb is in your heart, I know, and its wreath of flowers shall not fade." And the mother wept joyful tears as she pressed her child closely to her bosom, silently asking a blessing on her head. And the mother's daily prayers, and the child's constant endeavors to do well were not in vain, for Rosa became such a delight, such a blessing to all around her, that she gained the name of "Lammie."

# LILLA'S DREAM.

**B**EAUTIFUL was the May morning that Lilla, with joyful steps and innocent delight, strolled over the pastures and through the woods. She ran about over the moss-covered rocks, and plucked the gay columbines that bent at their sides for shelter. She walked by the sparkling brook, and threw herself down amongst the violets that decked its borders, and her ear was delighted with the joyous gurgling of its waters, and with the cheerful melody of the spring birds, and the drowsy hum of the newly-awakened insects. She returned

home with her basket full of flowers, and
her heart and mind full of those beautiful
feelings and thoughts which good angels
delight to infuse into the minds of little
children; and laying herself on her couch,
she fell into a sweet sleep, and she dreamed
that she was walking in a garden of fruit
trees, and that it was the joyous spring-
time of the year; and though there were
various kinds of trees in the garden, such
as the apple, the pear, the peach, and the
plum, also many kinds which Lilla's waking
eye had never seen, yet they were all in
full bloom. The peach trees bore pink
blossoms; the plum, cherry, and pear trees,
white; and so full of blossoms were the
trees, that she could scarcely see any green
leaves. The ground beneath the trees was

covered with flowers of almost every hue; and the blossoms looked so glad, that Lilla wondered they did not sing out for joy, as the birds and insects did.

That moment, a honey-bee that was buzzing near a rose-bush, whispered in her ear, and said, "They do sing; they are at this moment singing a joyous song in concert, but your senses are too gross to perceive it; I can hear it, and I can understand all their words."

"Oh!" cried Lilla, "I wish I were a honey-bee, that I too might hear it!" and she stood still, and listened very intently, scarcely daring to breathe. Soon she thought her hearing had grown more clear, and she could distinctly perceive a sound like the far-off tinkling of little bells, and

5

her heart leaped for joy. Breathless, she
continued to listen, till at length she could
even distinguish the words, and their song
was that of gladness and gratitude for their
existence. Lilla listened a long time in
delight, and then she went and sat down on
a little green mound to rest. While she
sat there, a frog came hopping up the
bank; Lilla was about to frighten him
away, but he looked up into her face with
an expression of so much kindness, that
she thought it seemed to say, "come near,
little maid, let us be friends;" and he
smiled roughly with his great mouth; and
she said, "Speckled-sides, why do you not
sing like the birds? you have a mouth big
enough; and even the blossoms on the
trees are singing this bright spring morn-

ing, and yet you are silent; what right have you to take up your abode in this place, so full of melody, if you cannot sing?"

" Indeed!" exclaimed Speckled-sides, tossing up his head, and looking mighty proud, "do but follow me to the nearest brook, where my companions are holding a concert, and you will soon see;" and he turned from her, and hopped down the bank as fast as he could go.

Lilla followed him into a deep meadow, through which ran the pretty streamlet. The ground all round the brook was blue with violets, and they sang the same song as did the blossoms in the garden. This meadow was a sunny place; there were trees to shelter it from the wind on every side, but so far off, that their shadows did not reach the spot where Lilla stood, and the warm sun-beams felt pleasantly as they fell upon her neck. Speckled-sides leaped into the brook, and, sitting up as straight as he could, so that his head might be seen out of the water, joined his loud voice with those of the other frogs. Lilla perceived that the song of the frogs did not glide from their mouths in graceful undulations, like those of the birds, but that it was monotonous and discordant, yet did it delight her soul. It seemed like the warmth of the sun-beams; it gave her the idea of newly awakened life, and warmth, and joy.

"It is the song," said she, "which always brings to mind the thoughts of spring, that season of returning life and gladness;

I love to listen to it, for there is music even in its monotony;" and she laid herself down upon the bed of blue violets by the side of the brook, as she had done in the morning; and as she lay there, she saw nothing but the blue sky; she heard the voices of birds around and above her, but she saw them not; and it seemed as if the sky came down nearer and nearer to her, or that she was lifted up towards it, and the voices of the birds seemed like the voices of invisible spirits, singing around her. She saw nothing but beauty; she heard nothing but song; she felt nothing but the pleasant warmth of the sunbeams; and her little heart was full of joy and love. She turned her face toward the brook which flowed through the meadow in various windings, leaping over bright pebbles, which sparkled in the sunlight like gems.

"Little brook," said she, "whither art thou going? Perhaps thou canst not tell thyself, beautiful brook!"

"I am free! I am free!" cried the brook; "and I know not, neither do I care, whither I go. I have been chained up all winter, with a cold, cold chain; and now that I am free, I will run without stopping, till Jack Frost binds me again."

"Then," said Lilla, "I will follow and see;" and she ran along by the side of the brook, which led her through many flowery meadows, and at length into a deep dell. When Lilla had followed it down the steep, and stood at the bottom of the dell, her little soul was full of wonder; and clasping her hands in a transport of delight, she exclaimed, "this must be heaven or some fairy land." The ground and all the rocks were covered with moss of the most brilliant green, and it felt as soft to her little feet as a velvet cushion; and the sun, which was shining over her head through the foliage, was luminous — yet it was not like daylight, nor was it like moonlight; it shone with a green brilliancy, so that everything in the dell gleamed like liquid emeralds. There were many beautiful flowers growing up out of the green moss, and beautiful birds singing among the trees; the squirrels and the green lizards ran along the branches. Down at the very bottom of the dell, there was a large flat rock covered with red cup moss ; some of these fairy goblets were standing half full of dew, and others were thrown over on their sides, and some of them were broken ; there were also berries and broken nuts scattered about the rock. Presently a squirrel jumped up and began to gather them ; then Lilla approached, and took one of the goblets ; the squirrel looked up into her face, and smilingly said, " Good morning." He then took a goblet, and asked politely if she would drink some dew with him ; and they drank off their cups together.

" Pray tell me, Nut-cracker," said Lilla, " what company has been feasting here on this rock ; these broken goblets seem to tell of high glee and festivity."

" Why, the fairies, the fairies, to be

sure; dost thou not know the fairy goblets? This dell belongs to king Oberon and queen Titania, and joyous indeed are the revels they hold here."

" I should like to see one of the fairies," said Lilla.

" Come with me," said Nut-cracker, " and I will show you one."

So he went leaping along over the green moss, and as Lilla ran after, it seemed to her that she was flying, so fast did she have to run that she might keep pace with him. He led her into an open part of the dell, where the trees were not so thick, and where the ground was entirely covered with flowers of almost every hue.

" There is Dew-drop, a very pretty fairy," said Nut-cracker, pointing to a sylph-like figure in the midst of the flowers.

"Let us go," said Lilla, "and see what she is doing."

So they went to the fairy, and they said, "What dost thou with the flowers, pretty being? thou dost not seem to be plucking them."

"Do you see the beautiful figures on these flowers?" asked the fairy.

"Oh! yes," replied Lilla.

"Well," said the fairy, "they have a meaning which, perhaps, you have not dreamed of; these pencilings are musical notes, and *we* alone can understand them — and we sing our songs from them. There are about the flowers great mysteries; on some of them are beautiful stories, and the songs which we sing are here written — and when we learn them, we

write them on the brain of some sleeping
mortal whose soul delights in melodies;
when he awakes he gives them forth to the
world. The stories we write on the brain,
as we said, but the mysteries we keep to
ourselves."

"Oh!" said Lilla, "make me to understand the notes, that I may sing more
sweetly than the birds."

Then the fairy taught her one of the
songs, and it seemed in her dream as if she
lifted up her voice and sang. Louder and
louder it grew, till she seemed to fill the
whole air with her music.

Then Dew-drop asked Lilla if she would
like to go and amuse herself in the Elfin's
Cave; and as she did not know what sort
of a place this was, she was curious to see

it, and requested Dew-drop to guide her thither. Now Dew-drop called two of her torch-bearers, the fire-flies, to light them through the dark cave.

They went on together, and when they had entered the cave, Dew-drop said — "Now we will amuse ourselves. Thou seest how rocky are the sides of the cave. This rock is soft and flaky, like slate-stone, and is very easily split apart; let us open some of it, and see what we can find between the flakes." And by the light of the fire-flies they began to split the flaky rock, and to the great surprise of Lilla, they found between the flakes beautiful pictures of every description. She also found musical notes, which they sang, and the hollow cave echoed to their voices. After Lilla had looked at everything she could find, they left the cave; and Dew-drop, bidding her good morning, returned to the flowers.

"Lilla!" cried a little voice from the branches of an apple-tree, under which she stood.

She looked up, and espied the smiling face of Nut-cracker, looking down upon her through the foliage; he was sitting on a bough of the tree, holding in his little paws an apple, from which he was picking out the seeds and eating them. He threw down one of the apples to Lilla, who, at Nut-cracker's request, began to save her seeds. While she was picking them out, she said to them:

"Poor prisoners! what a miserable life you must lead, shut up in the very centre of this dark apple."

"No matter," answered they, "we are content; we do not live for ourselves; yesterday was for the sake of to-day, and to-day for the sake of to-morrow; and we are formed for the sake of the tree which now lies in embryo within us. Unlike selfish human beings, all we desire is, that the end of our existence may be answered."

Lilla walked away, and seeing an apple-tree in full blossom, she said, — "This tree and its fair blossoms live for themselves, no doubt."

"Nay," answered the tree, "I draw nourishment from the earth, and spread out my leaves that they may receive heat and life from the sun; the showers of rain are for the sake of the fruit we bear; we clothe ourselves in blossoms, because they are the means of producing seed."

" Yes," said the blossoms, " we are content to wither and drop off as soon as our task is done ; for it is for the sake of the fruit that we exist, and our fruit for the sake of man ; so, when our fruit is eaten, the seeds are free to mix themselves in the mould, in order to send forth another tree."

Lilla left the tree, and presently came to a part of the dell where the flowery vines were climbing up and stretching themselves from limb to limb, forming a soft hammock, or cradle ; and, climbing up one of the trees, she leaped into the flowery hammock, and the wind came and rocked her to and fro so high that she was thrown out of it, and the sudden fright awoke her. She opened her eyes, and found her sister was shaking her, instead of the wind.

# THE CHILD'S DREAM

## AMONG FLOWERS.

BY MISS COLMAN.

WAVING sweetly o'er thy head,
 Flowers softly sigh;
Watching o'er thy grassy bed,
 Singing lullaby.

"Gently murmuring in thine ear,
 Angels from on high,
Resting in these lovely flowers,
 Sing thee lullaby.

"Bending o'er thee, darling child.
Kissing thy blue eye,
Singing softly to thy soul,
Sweetest lullaby."

Thus sang the flowers to the child, as he slept beneath their waving bells; and he heard them, and listened to the lullaby of the angels. The flowers watched him as he listened, and saw how beautiful smiles played over his face, and then, how tear-drops chased each other down his fair cheek, and how he again smiled peacefully; and they grew curious, wishing to know why the child smiled and wept by turns. And they sang to him again : —

6

"Child, among us lying,
　And so softly sleeping,
　Time is swiftly flying,
　Waken from thy dreaming.

"While thy mouth is smiling,
　And thy blue eyes beaming,
　While the sun is shining,
　Tell us of thy dreaming."

Then the child awakened; and he told the flowers how angels sat each side of him, and sang to him of his mother and sisters, who lived in heaven, and how happy they were; and how beautiful heaven was, and how he might go there and live; this made him feel very happy. But then the angels told him, with sweet, sad voices, how naughty he was, and how much he must do to be good enough to live in heaven; and his heart sank, and he feared that he *never* should see his dear mother again. Then he wept; — but soon he felt on his brow other tears, and he looked up, and saw the angels weeping. Then they sang to him again: —

"Weep not, weep not, darling child,
   We are ever near thee,
And, 'mid all the ills around,
   We will guard and help thee.

"And when thou art very good,
   In our arms we 'll take thee,
And, while singing thankful songs,
   Up to heaven we 'll bear thee."

Then the angels told him how he must watch the flowers, and listen to the birds,

— and they would teach him to be good;
but that he must pray often and heartily,
or else they could not stay with him.
Then they sang once more about heaven —
and how he would go there too; and they
kissed him on the forehead, softly and
gently, like the touch of a flower. Then
the flowers awoke him, — and now he had
told them what he had been dreaming.

And the flowers wept too at the lovely
dream of the beautiful child; and they
touched him with their bells as the angels
kissed him, and showered upon him dew-
drops, till his golden hair sparkled with
the liquid diamonds. Then the child felt
strong and hopeful; — and kneeling down
among the flowers, he prayed that he might
be good and pure, so that the angels would
take him soon to his mother.

# CHILDHOOD.

My heart leaps up when I behold
A rainbow in the sky;
So was it when my life began,
So is it now I am a man,
So let it be when I grow old,
Or let me die.          *Wordsworth.*

HE angel that takes care of the tender lambs and sprinkles dew upon the flowers in the still night, take care of thee, dear child, and let no evil come to thy tender years. Fair child! when I gaze into thy soft blue eyes *my* childhood returns, like a bright vision, and I think of the time, long since past, when every sight and

every sound in nature gave to me such
sweet delight, and all was *so* fair and beauti-
· ful. I fancy I hear thy gentle voice breath-
ing forth thy joy, in sweet and happy words,
such as little children are wont to use when
they first begin to look up into the blue
sky, to gaze upon the *rainbow*, or at the
bright, fleecy clouds that float over the
m on. The bright sun, the moon, and the
stars — the murmuring rivulet — the broad
ocean, heaving to and fro in the sunlight —
the pealing thunder, and the storm — the
quiet glen, where I listened to the busy
hum of the insects, the joyous song of the
birds, as they sung in the trees or flew from
spray to spray, the odor of fresh flowers
— *all* filled my breast with heavenly love
and peace ; and when I look up into thy

face, dear child, my soul returns to join you, and I forget the present, and live, for a time, only in the past. * * * * *

The little maid you see gazing at the great dragon-fly, is the foster child of a good shepherd; she has risen with the morning sun, and has come forth into the silent wood, to lift up her little voice, with the birds, in songs of praise and thanksgiving to the Creator, and to ask His blessing on all that lives. The little lamb by her side is the companion of all her walks; she gives it fresh grass to eat, with her own hand, and water from the clear stream that flows rippling beneath the green trees. She makes garlands of the choicest flowers, and hangs them upon his neck. She loves the flowers, the green grass, and the rip-

7

pling stream. She loves to walk with her
lamb in the still woods, and listen to the
hum of the little insects that dwell there.
She is Nature's happy child, and her dis-
courses are with its wonders. It is in the
quiet dell, by the softly murmuring stream,
that she loves most to stay; she is talking
now with that large dragon-fly; and if a
picture could speak, we should hear her say,
in the gentlest accents in the world:

" Come here, pretty dragon-fly, come
and rest on my hand, and let me feel of
your gossamer wings, and look into your
bright eyes; come, listen to me, and I will
tell you a tale — I will — "

But the dragon-fly hears her not — he is
looking at a beautiful lily, in whose soft
cup he intends to rest awhile — oh! how

beautiful it is! and the dragon-fly has lit upon it — the little maid claps her hands for joy, for she is sure of him now; and she stretches out her hand to the lily cup; but ere she could touch it, the pretty creature has flown from the flower, and as it pauses in the air, we can imagine that it says:

"Good-by, little girl, I shall not suffer myself to be caught to-day;" and off he flies, soaring higher and higher into the blue heavens.

MRS. COLMAN.

# THE KING OF THE SWANS:

## OR DELPHINE THE GOOD.

**FROM THE GERMAN.**

THERE was once a little girl, who was called Delphine, so good and cheerful, that she was a favorite with everybody. This good girl had a friend called Hilda, who was also a good girl, and they loved each other dearly.

In the winter, when the snow was lying deep upon hill and field, Hilda fell sick, and her parents were in great anxiety on her account. She was quite unable to eat — was burning with fever heat, and shivering with cold, by turns, — and though she was tenderly nursed, could get no relief.

If any of her young friends visited her, she would say to them, " *Give me straw-berries*, who will go and find me some strawberries, that I may get well and not die ? " Then her father and mother would say, " Dear Hilda, it is winter now, and there are none to be found this season."

Hilda would then raise herself up in bed, and say, " Far away over the high hill there, and through the forest, is a green slope ; there I can see plenty of straw-berries.

" Who will go and fetch them for me — only one of those nice red berries — only one ! " The children left the room, saying, to each other, " What nonsense poor Hilda

talked about; she must be dreaming."
But Delphine was much troubled that she
could not help her friend. All at once she
said, "Who will go with me over the moun-
tains to seek for strawberries? It will be
some comfort to poor Hilda if she sees
us going over the hill to seek for them."
But no one would go with her.

So Delphine set out alone, for she
wished to do all she could to help her
friend, though she had to go through a
deep and dangerous forest. After she left
the forest, she came to the hill. A small
trodden foot-path led up to the top and
down again on the other side; she then
came to a wood of tall oak and beach
trees. She passed through without having
met a single adventure; she then came to

a place where three paths met. She stood
still a moment, not knowing which to take,
when, quite unexpectedly, she saw a little
man approaching through the trees. He
had a green hat upon his head, with a
feather as white as snow. His dress was
made of the softest swan's down. He car-
ried an ivory bow on his shoulder, and a
small silver hunting horn hung at his side.
"What do you want here, little damsel?"
he said, in a friendly voice.

"Ah!" said Delphine, "I have a sick
friend, who longs for strawberries, and says
they will make her well again. I know
very well that it is winter, but I hope to
find something here that she will like, and
I hope that I shall not return quite empty-
handed."

"Come with me then," said the little
hunter. "I will show you a place where
you may find what you are in search of."
He went on before, leading her through
many winding paths, until the forest appeared lighter, the air warmer and more
spring-like. At last they came to a great
iron door. The little man unlocked it,
saying, "Now, if you go straight forward,
you will find what you seek."

Delphine would have thanked the good
man, but he vanished instantly. After
walking a few steps farther, she came to a
green slope.

Here winter had entirely disappeared.
The sun shone warmer in the cloudless
sky; the birds sang merrily, and a few
steps farther she beheld the ground covered

with fine strawberries. How the good little maiden rejoiced! she quickly filled the little basket she brought with her, and hastened back with them to her dear sick friend. But some how in her haste she could not find her way back. She came to the iron palisades which surrounded the place, but all her attempts to find the gate were fruitless. In her anxiety, she ran this way and that; still no gate was to be seen. Then she heard the sound of a whistle, and she exclaimed, with joy, "I hear a living sound, some one, surely, is in this wood who will be kind enough to show me the way out."

She hastily traversed the thicket in another direction, and suddenly beheld a scene which caused her great surprise.

Before her laid a large, green meadow, and
beyond this a clear lake, on which a num-
ber of stately and beautiful swans were
swimming very gracefully.    In the middle
of the lake was a small island, upon which
stood a charming palace, surrounded by
flower gardens and orange groves.    As she
drew near the shore of the lake, she perceived a little man, who had a less friendly
aspect than the hunter of the forest.    He
had a large head, with rough hair, and a
grey beard, so long that it reached to his
knees ; in one hand he held a whistle, and
in the other a switch.

Delphine was afraid to speak to him, and
stood still, at a little distance.    She soon
observed that his office was to take care of
the swans, and prevent their going out of

the water. When any did so, he whistled
to them, and if they did not obey him,
he stretched out his switch, which* had
the remarkable property of lengthening or
shortening—just as he wished to have it.
Delphine could see no one save this little
old man, nor any mode of reaching the
palace; therefore she gained courage to
say, "Good friend, can you show me how
to get out of the forest? I wish to go
home." The grey-beard looked at her in
surprise, but did not speak; he merely
made her understand, by signs, that she
should sit down, which she did.

Then he whistled, and presently there
came a large swan from the lake, which
laid itself down before him. The little old
man seated himself on the swan's back,

throwing one of his arms round its neck, and away the trusty bird swam with him across the lake ; there he alighted, and went into the palace. Delphine waited some time, curious to see what would happen, but she did not feel afraid. At length she saw four black swans swim from a creek of the lake, harnessed to a beautiful little green boat, adorned with silver, and shaded by a pair of wings, which covered the seats ; the front was in shape like a swan's neck.

The grey-beard sat there, looking much more agreeable than before. He gave Delphine a sign to step in, which she did ; they then sailed gently across the lake, and as soon as they reached the other side, he handed her out and led her to the palace.

In the hall, sat the King of the Swans. He wore a robe of the purest white silk, bordered with swan's down; a golden crown was upon his head, and he was surrounded by richly dressed attendants.

"What dost thou seek in my kingdom?" inquired he.

"I have found all I sought," answered Delphine; "but I pray your majesty to let some one of your attendants direct me home, for I find I have wandered in the wrong direction."

"Very well," said the King, "what hast thou to offer?"

"Alas!" replied Delphine, "I have nothing at all. If I had known what you would have wished of me, I should have brought it with me from home."

"Thou hast strawberries," rejoined the King, "and I like them above all things. Give me thy strawberries, and then one of my servants shall show thee the way home."

"Alas! I cannot give thee all," continued Delphine; "they are for my sick friend, who must die if she does not get them; but I will willingly give you some of them."

She then took several of the finest looking ones, and tied them by the stems with a riband that confined her hair, and handed them to the King.

"Thank my little daughter," said the King. "Now go thy way, and this man shall attend thee; but do exactly as he desires."

The old man with the grey beard waited in readiness for her, and when Delphine had taken leave of the King, he led her into the garden, tied a handkerchief about her eyes, whistled, and at the same instant took her by the arm.

She heard the rustling of wings, she felt the wind blow colder and colder, in her face, but was not conscious of moving, nor could she see anything.

At last the sound of wings ceased, and the old man set her upon the ground. " Now, my child, count twenty, and then remove the bandage and preserve it carefully; it will be required of thee at the proper time."

As soon as the bandage was removed, she found herself standing on the hill, opposite the house of her friend, Hilda.

Then she hastened to her friend, who was still in bed repeating the words, " *Who will bring me strawberries to make me well* ? "

" There they are, dear Hilda," said Delphine, handing her a bright red bunch.⁊ Every one was astonished, and anxious to know from whence she had brought them. But she had barely begun to relate her wonderful adventures, before Hilda had eaten all the strawberries. Then the color returned to her face, and strength to her limbs ; and Hilda said, " Thank the Lord, and dear Delphine, now I am quite well ! " And she rose from her bed, quite restored.

Who can tell how the parents thanked and blessed Delphine — the good, kind-hearted Delphine, whom every one praised and blessed — for her self-sacrificing benevolence and love ?

One day, when Delphine was walking in the meadows with her mother, some years after this, and was looking up into the sky, she saw a black speck, which, as it descended, grew larger and larger; and as it came towards her, she saw that it was a prodigious black swan. It had on its back a tent, with golden gauze curtains, and when it alighted upon the ground where Delphine was standing, there came out of the tent a little man, with friendly eyes, who thus addressed her, "I am the King of the *Swans.* I have heard that you will, in a short time, celebrate a joyful festival; and as thou gavest me a present when a child, and hast grown up so good, brave, and pure a maiden, I will make thee a present in return." Saying these words,

8

he put upon her head a costly crown. It was made of gold, garnished with strawberry leaves; and between the leaves there sparkled red rubies, diamonds, and purple amethysts; round the rim was a beautiful gold band.

Delphine and her mother could hardly thank the King, for astonishment. But he did not give them time, for the swan rose majestically in the air, and soon became as a little black spot in the midst of the bright clouds.

Many a little boy and girl have gone over the hill, since that time, to seek the land of the Swans, in search of strawberries in winter, but have not found them; perhaps it was because they were *more selfish,* and not so good as *Delphine.*

# CORINNE.

ILD broke the morning,
  The meadows looked gay,
The birds sweetly caroled
  The welcome of May;
And blithely the girls played
  At ball on the green,
But the sweetest, the fairest,
  Was little Corinne.

.

At hoop and at rope
  She was first of the throng,
And sweet as the lark
  Of the woodland her song;

None who saw the curls fall
    O'er her forehead so fair,
Could doubt the calm picture
    Of innocence there.

Dance gaily along,
    Ever joyous and free,
Less joyous and happy,
    Oh! ne'er may'st thou be;
Young, artless, and lovely,
    Still bright be the scene,
Ever blessed with thy presence,
    My pretty Corinne.

# COUSIN LU-LU BOOKS,

ORIGINAL AND SELECTED ... BY MISS COLMAN.

## PUBLISHED BY HOWE & FERRY.

NEW YORK

## LU-LU ALPHABET,

ARRANGED AS A STORY,

## WITH NUMEROUS PICTURES.

## LU-LU MULTIPLIER,

OR FIRST LESSONS IN MULTIPLICATION,

IN SIMPLE RHYME,

CONTAINING THIRTY-TWO PICTURES.

New Stories for Girls.

New Stories for Boys.

} Intended especially for little folks, and are of a playful and moral character.

Stories for Children.

Poetry for Children.

} For those rather more advanced in learning.

The Series comprises Six Books named above, printed on good paper, and neatly bound with illuminated covers, or in cloth—and sold at low prices.

# COUSIN LU-LU GAMES,

## COMPRISE

## THE ALPHABET DISSECTED,

### ON THIRTY CARDS, HANDSOMELY COLORED,

And put up in a neat strong box.

## THE MULTIPLIER, DISSECTED,

### ON TWENTY-EIGHT CARDS, HANDSOMELY COLORED,

And put up in a neat strong box.

---

# YOUTH'S LETTER WRITER,

### OR THE EPISTOLATORY ART MADE PLAIN AND EASY TO BEGINNERS, THROUGH THE EXAMPLE OF HENRY MORETON.

## By Mrs. John Farrar, of Cambridge.

This little Book is designed to assist young people in the first attempt at Writing Letters.

" We therefore recommend the work, not only as the completest, but most readable Letter Writer which is to be had at the Book-stores."—CHRISTIAN EXAMINER.

www.ingramcontent.com/pod-product-compliance
Lightning Source LLC
Chambersburg PA
CBHW031441270326

41930CB00007B/818

* 9 7 8 3 3 3 7 0 0 5 2 4 5 *